source to resource

FROM SUNSHINE TO LIGHTBULB

MICHAEL BRIGHT

WAYLAND
www.waylandbooks.co.uk

Contents

Electricity grid

Essential Sun

Solar energy is light and heat from the **Sun**. It keeps us **warm**, helps us to grow food to **eat** and affects our weather. We can use the Sun's **energy** to generate **electricity** via solar cells, like the ones on this house. The electricity is fed into the home. Any extra electricity that is not used will be passed back to the national electricity grid.

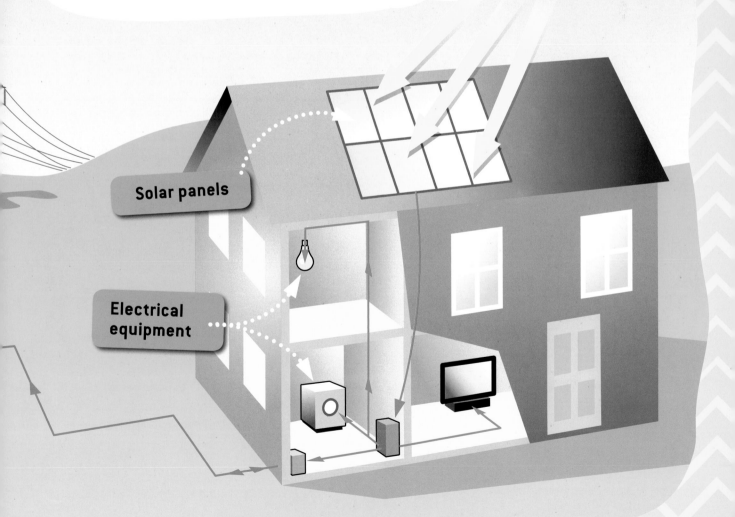

Solar panels

Electrical equipment

The Sun and our Earth

Solar energy is said to be a 'renewable' energy source because somewhere on Earth it is always available and it never runs out. Oil, coal and natural gas are 'non-renewable' because one day they will be gone completely.

The Sun and people

Energy from the Sun is vital for life on Earth. Plants need sunlight to grow, animals need to eat plants and we, in turn, need to eat plants and animals to survive. Without the Sun, there would be no plants, no animals and no people.

Winds and waves

The Sun also powers the weather. It heats up the oceans and atmosphere closer to the equator more than at the poles. Hot air rises and cold air from cold regions rushes in to replace it, producing winds that whip up waves.

Cows eat grass, and grass needs sunlight to grow.

Two other renewable energy sources are also generated by the Sun — wind and wave power.

Sun worship

Many ancient civilisations realised how important the Sun was to their very survival, so they worshipped it. A major Egyptian sun god was Ra. His eye was the glowing disc of the Sun, and he represented light, warmth and growth.

Rain and rivers

Heat from the Sun causes clouds to form over the oceans. These clouds drop rain on to the land. The water flows into rivers that fill reservoirs. The movement of water out of reservoirs can be used to generate electricity. This is called hydroelectric power, and it is another renewable energy source that has its origins in the Sun.

The Sun

Our Sun is a star at the centre of our solar system. It is 1,300,000 times bigger than the Earth, and consists mainly of two gases called hydrogen and helium.

Multi-layered Sun

The Sun is made up of many layers of gas and plasma. The temperature at the Sun's core is a staggering 15,000,000°C.

The **solar prominences** are great loops and fountains in the corona.

The **core** is the Sun's engine room, where solar energy is generated.

BRAINY BITS

The **radiation zone** moves the heat quickly from the core to the next layer, the convection zone.

The **convection zone** is like a boiling pot. It moves the heat more slowly from the radiation zone to the photosphere.

The **corona** is the crown-like, wispy outer layer of the Sun that can be seen around the Sun's disc during a total eclipse.

The **photosphere** is the surface of the Sun, where light is released. Surprisingly, it can take several thousand years for heat to travel from the core to the Sun's surface.

The **chromosphere** is a layer of gas about 2,000 km thick above the Sun's surface. It gives out red light.

The Sun can warm the Earth, even though it is very far away.

How the Sun works

Solar energy begins in the Sun's core. Here, tiny subatomic particles slam together in a process known as 'nuclear fusion'. This produces most of the heat and light given off by the Sun.

The Sun's life span

The Sun formed about 4.6 billion years ago from a vast cloud of gas and dust in space. Today, it is described as being 'middle-aged', so it is unlikely to change very much for another 4 billion years.

Clever Copernicus

Before the sixteenth century, it was thought that the Earth was the centre of the universe and that the Sun revolved around it. All that changed in 1530 CE. The Polish astronomer Nicolaus Copernicus said that the Earth circles the Sun, which is the centre of our solar system. He was right!

Sunlight's journey to Earth

The Sun is about 150 million kilometres away, so heat and light from the Sun must travel this great distance through space to reach the Earth. But it does not take long. On average, sunlight arrives in 8 minutes and 20 seconds.

Energy through space

The journey may be quick but only a very small proportion of the Sun's energy actually reaches the Earth. Even so, there is more solar energy reaching the Earth every day than all the people on our planet could possibly use.

Reflected sunlight

Not all the sunlight that travels into the Earth's atmosphere reaches its surface. About a third is reflected back into space and lost. All surfaces reflect sunlight, even a black road, but snow, ice and the tops of clouds reflect the most.

Much of the Sun's heat and light is reflected back into space.

Clouds both reflect and absorb the Sun's rays, preventing them from reaching the planet's surface.

1/3 sunlight is reflected back into space.

1/3 sunlight absorbed by the atmosphere, oceans and land.

1/3 sunlight that reaches Earth and is available to generate electricity.

Absorbed sunlight

The atmosphere, oceans and land absorb a third of the sunlight that is not reflected. In fact, they absorb more of the Sun's energy in one hour than the amount of energy we all use in an entire year. It means that only a third of the sunlight reaching Earth is available to be used generate electricity.

Worldwide impact

Power production is something all the countries of the world need to consider. Some forms of energy generation, such as coal, oil or natural gas, produce the 'greenhouse' gas carbon dioxide. The more carbon dioxide that enters the atmosphere through the use of these forms of power generation, the more the planet warms and ice melts. There is less ice to reflect away sunlight and the planet warms even more – a process called 'the runaway greenhouse'. The reflection of sunlight is important to global warming and climate change. It is hoped that solar power may one day replace these other forms of power generation, and help to slow down, or even stop, the ice from melting. This, in turn, may reduce the impact of the greenhouse effect.

Electricity from sunlight

Electricity is converted directly from sunlight using solar cells. Modern solar cells were first invented in the twentieth century, although the science behind them was discovered a hundred years earlier.

How do they work?

Solar cells are made from thin layers of a chemical called silicon. When sunlight hits the silicon it generates an electric field across the layers. The electricity can be drawn off and used to power electrical equipment.

When do they work?

Solar cells only work well when the Sun is out. They are very dependent on the weather. On a dull day, they produce less electricity than on a sunny day, and they do not work at night.

Small solar cells like this can be found in calculators, but larger ones make up roof panels.

Many solar cells joined together are called solar panels or modules. Several panels joined together form an array that can produce lots of electricity.

🕐 Timeline

1839 Alexander Edmond Becquerel discovers how sunlight can be converted into electricity.

1941 Russell Ohl invents the solar cell.

1954 Bell Labs produces the first useful silicon solar cell. Previous ones had been too inefficient.

1958 Vanguard I space satellite uses solar power in space for the first time.

1967 Soyuz 1 is the first manned spacecraft powered by solar cells.

1978 The first solar-powered calculators are invented.

2014 The solar-powered space probe, Philae, lands on a comet.

Solar-powered satellites

One of the first uses of solar cells was to power satellites in space. The early satellites were spheres with solar cells attached to the side. Later satellites and space probes, including the International Space Station, have large panels of solar cells resembling an aircraft's wings.

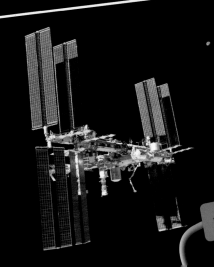

Solar panels

At first, solar cells were expensive to produce, but over the years they have become cheaper to manufacture. This means people all over the world have begun to use solar panels on homes and buildings. Households can then generate their own electricity, and even sell some back to the energy companies.

Homes usually have their solar panels on the roof.

Solar farms

People in local communities get together and use fields and other open spaces, such as factory roofs, for large arrays of solar panels. The panels can even swivel as they track the Sun across the sky.

One of the largest is the Solar Star in California, USA. It has 1.7 million solar panels spread over 13 square kilometres of the Mojave Desert.

Solar power stations

On a bigger scale, solar power stations generate large amounts of electricity to be fed into the main electricity supply.

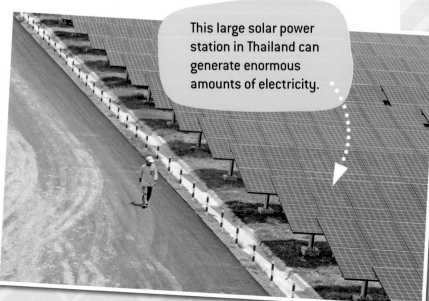

This large solar power station in Thailand can generate enormous amounts of electricity.

The National Stadium in Taiwan is the world's largest sports stadium to be powered almost entirely by solar energy.

Solar design

Some designers are creating solar arrays that blend in with the environment around them. One of the first was the Space Ark in Japan. The structure of 5,046 solar panels is built in the shape of a floating ark.

Solar architecture

Modern solar arrays are being included on important buildings, too. One of the most striking is the National Stadium in Taiwan. Its roof is covered in 8,844 solar panels – enough to supply 1,000 homes with electricity if it was part of the national grid.

Solar on the street

Small solar panels are used to illuminate road traffic signs. Many have batteries to store the electricity generated during the day to light up the signs at night. Solar energy can also be used for street lighting in remote areas.

DID YOU KNOW?

If just a small area of the Sahara was covered with solar panels, it could generate enough electricity for the entire world.

Electricity reaching homes

The electricity from solar panels, whether it is from rooftop arrays on the top of homes, solar farms or solar power stations, is used directly by the home or fed into the regional and national power supply. The power companies distribute it nationally and even internationally.
It follows this process:

BRAINY BITS

3 Transformer substation
The electricity passes through a step-up transformer so that it is a higher voltage for travelling long distances. A large amount of electricity at low voltage would be lost as heat over a long distance, but this loss is reduced at higher voltages.

2 Inverter
Electricity from solar cells is direct current (DC) so it has to be converted into alternating current (AC) before it can be used. AC is used because it can be increased or decreased by a transformer.

1 Generator
The electricity is generated in various ways, including by solar farms and solar power stations.

4 Transmission lines

High voltage transmission lines strung between towers or pylons carry the electricity across the country to cities and villages. Some cables may run underground or lie on the bottom of the sea.

The longest

The world's longest undersea transmission line is between Norway and the Netherlands in the North Sea. The undersea part is 580 kilometres long.

5 Transformer substation

Here a step-down transformer reduces the voltage to make it safe for use in the home.

The tallest

The world's tallest power transmission towers support overhead cables between Damao Island and Liangmao Island in China. The two towers are 370 metres tall.

6 Transmission lines

Low voltage transmission lines carry the electricity to a street. They might be overhead lines in the country or underground in the city.

Electricity use

Most of us take electricity for granted. We flick a switch and the lights turn on. Today, more and more people around the world are using electricity, and electricity use is rising at an enormous rate.

Earth lights

It is only from the International Space Station orbiting the Earth that the full extent of electricity use across the world can be seen. Cities across the globe are blazes of artificial light. It is also possible to see remote areas of Earth where little electricity is used.

The grid

All the electricity distribution lines across countries and, in some cases, over entire continents, are interconnected. By sharing the electricity, the power companies make sure it goes to where it is needed most. These networks are known as 'national grids' or 'power grids'.

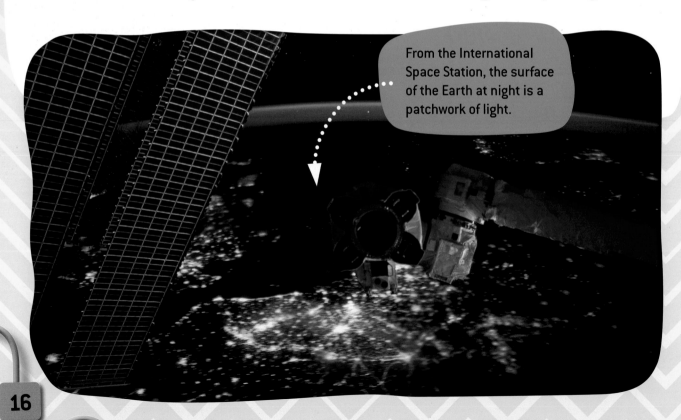

From the International Space Station, the surface of the Earth at night is a patchwork of light.

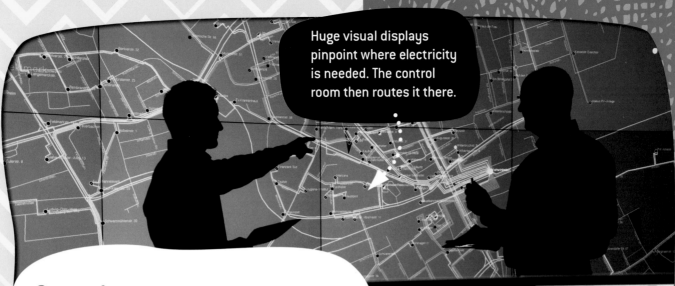

Huge visual displays pinpoint where electricity is needed. The control room then routes it there.

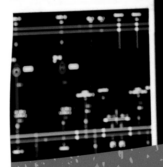

Control rooms

The companies that run power grids control the flow of electricity from large control rooms. They direct electricity around their own region and send it out to or bring it in from other regions.

Peak demand

In many countries, electricity use is highest at 5.30 in the evening when homes, offices and factories are all making heavy demands at the same time. Similar peaks occur on traditional feast days, such as Thanksgiving in the USA, when millions of domestic electric ovens are cooking at the same time.

Super grids

Increasingly, countries are working together to ensure that the lights stay on. In Europe and North Africa, for example, there are plans to connect up electricity networks to take advantage of the climate in different countries. Together, they will generate electricity from solar power, wind power and hydroelectric power. North Africa sees more sunshine than Europe, and northern Europe has more wind and plenty of water, so the two regions can generate and swap electricity. The network is called the 'SuperSmart Grid'.

Electricity in the home

Most homes get their electricity supply from the regional or national grid. Even solar-powered homes sometimes need to buy extra electricity from energy companies. However, a house can generate its own electricity with solar panels on the roof.

Electricity cables

When the cables from a supplier and from the solar panels enter the house, the electricity passes through several key stages:

Electricity meter

Electricity enters a house via an electricity meter. It records how much is used, and how much extra from the solar panel is sold back to the energy company.

Fuse box or service panel

Electricity from the mains and solar panels passes through a box with circuit breakers or fuses that switch off the electricity if there is danger.

Household circuits

Inside the fuse box or service panel, electricity is routed to separate circuits: upstairs lights, downstairs lights, electric cooker, upstairs sockets and downstairs sockets; each socket with its emergency circuit breaker or fuse.

The service panel master switch turns on and off the electricity supply.

One-fifth of electricity in the home is used for lighting.

Electrical circuits

On a lighting circuit, the electricity usually travels through wires hidden in the walls, floors or ceilings. It might go directly to a light fitting in the ceiling or on a wall. A plug-and-socket circuit allows you to connect an electrical device, such as a computer, to the main power supply.

DID YOU KNOW?

There are two main standards of electricity strength: 220–240 volts in Europe and 120 volts in the USA.

Global plugs

Plugs and sockets are different all over the world. Some plugs have round pins, others have flat pins and still others have rectangular pins. Here are just a few plugs and sockets and where they come from:

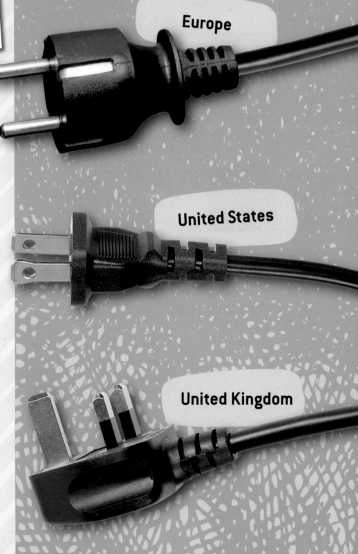

Europe

United States

United Kingdom

The light bulb

Before the late nineteenth century, lighting was fuelled by gas and oil. Gas lamps lit city streets and oil lamps and candles lit up homes. In 1879, all this began to change. The first mass produced electric light bulb was invented. It was called an incandescent light bulb.

How does it work?

The incandescent light bulb lights up when electricity passes through a wire filament. The filament heats up to a high temperature until it glows. It is protected within a glass 'bulb' that contains a gas or a vacuum. Unfortunately, these kinds of light bulbs are not very efficient. More than 95 per cent of the energy produces heat rather than light.

Halogen

In 1882, the halogen light bulb was invented, but a household version was not available until 1959. In a halogen light bulb, the filament is surrounded by halogen gas. The filament lasts longer and glows brighter with a whiter light. It can also be much smaller and requires less electricity compared to an incandescent light bulb with the same brightness. It is often used in security lights outside the house.

Energy-saving light bulbs

Lighting accounts for nearly 20 per cent of a household electricity bill, so many people are switching to 'compact fluorescent' light bulbs (CFLs) and 'light emitting diodes' (LEDs) to be less wasteful with electricity. Both are types of energy-saving light bulbs that are more efficient and use less electricity.

DID YOU KNOW?

In 1880, the electric light bulb was first used commercially not in the home or in an office or factory, but on a steamship – the SS *Columbia*.

Inventor of the light bulb

Thomas Edison was one of 24 scientists who invented the incandescent light bulb at about the same time. However, Edison is the person everybody remembers because his light bulb could be mass produced. He once said, "we will make electricity so cheap, that only the rich will burn candles".

Dim and bright

The brightness of a light bulb depends on its 'wattage'. Usually, the higher the wattage, the brighter the bulb and the more electricity it uses. However, energy-saving light bulbs have a lower wattage than incandescent bulbs. They use less electricity, but are just as bright.

Solar heating

Solar panels use sunlight to generate electricity. Other solar devices can capture the Sun's heat and be used to heat up water or air.

Solar water heating

The most common form of solar heating is the solar water heating system. It consists of a panel containing thin tubes filled with water, which is usually placed on the roof of a house. The Sun warms the water in the pipes and it is then sent to an insulated storage tank. More pipes may connect the tank to the house's central heating and hot water systems to warm rooms and feed baths and sinks. In warmer climates, solar hot water can provide about 85 per cent of a home's hot water needs.

There are two types of solar thermal panels: a flat plate panel with tiny tubes, and a larger tube version, like these, from which the air has been removed to reduce heat loss.

Buildings absorb heat from the Sun, which can be used to help warm the building.

Solar air heating

Special heat-absorbent materials can absorb the Sun's heat. The stored heat can be used to heat air being sucked into a building. A large panel or even an entire wall on the sunny side of a building might be used to absorb the Sun's heat. The warmed air is then pumped around the building in the air conditioning and heating systems.

Solar building design

Many modern buildings are being designed to maximise or minimise the use of the Sun's energy. The walls, windows and floors collect, store and distribute solar energy as heat in the winter, yet they make sure that less heat is absorbed in the summer. Large windows are a simple way to gain heat in winter, and shutters keep out the Sun in summer.

Danish island

The world's largest solar water heating systems are not found in a hot desert, but on the Danish island of Ærø. Here, solar energy accounts for 30 per cent of the island's annual heating needs, and this rises to 100 per cent between June and August. Also, giant wind turbines provide 50 per cent of its electricity, so the island gains most of its energy through renewable resources.

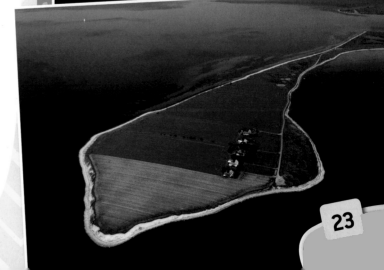

Solar towers and furnaces

Solar towers are used to capture the Sun's energy to heat water to generate electricity. Solar furnaces concentrate that energy to heat up furnaces to high temperatures.

How do they work?

Both these systems use mirrors that track the Sun across the sky and focus it on special towers. It works in a similar way to focusing light with a magnifying glass to burn a hole in paper.

Solar towers

A large number of flat mirrors focus sunlight on to a solar power tower. Inside the tower, a special heat-carrying fluid is heated to 500°C. This is pumped to a boiler and the heat used to produce steam. The steam drives a turbine that generates electricity.

All the mirrors direct the sunlight at the central solar tower, which glows white-hot.

Solar furnaces

Solar furnaces use curved mirrors to heat chemicals up to very high temperatures. In the Pyrenees, a mountainous region in Europe, a solar furnace was built in a specific location because the area has about 300 sunny days a year.

Solar barbecues and ovens

Small, portable solar barbecues and ovens are being used in remote areas of poorer countries. They concentrate the Sun's rays to cook food and boil water, without the need to collect firewood.

Solar bowl

At Auroville in India, a large solar bowl is used as a solar kitchen. The huge bowl-shaped mirror focuses sunlight on to a cylindrical boiler, heating the water inside to 150°C. The steam produced is enough to cook large quantities of food, giving 1,000 people two meals a day.

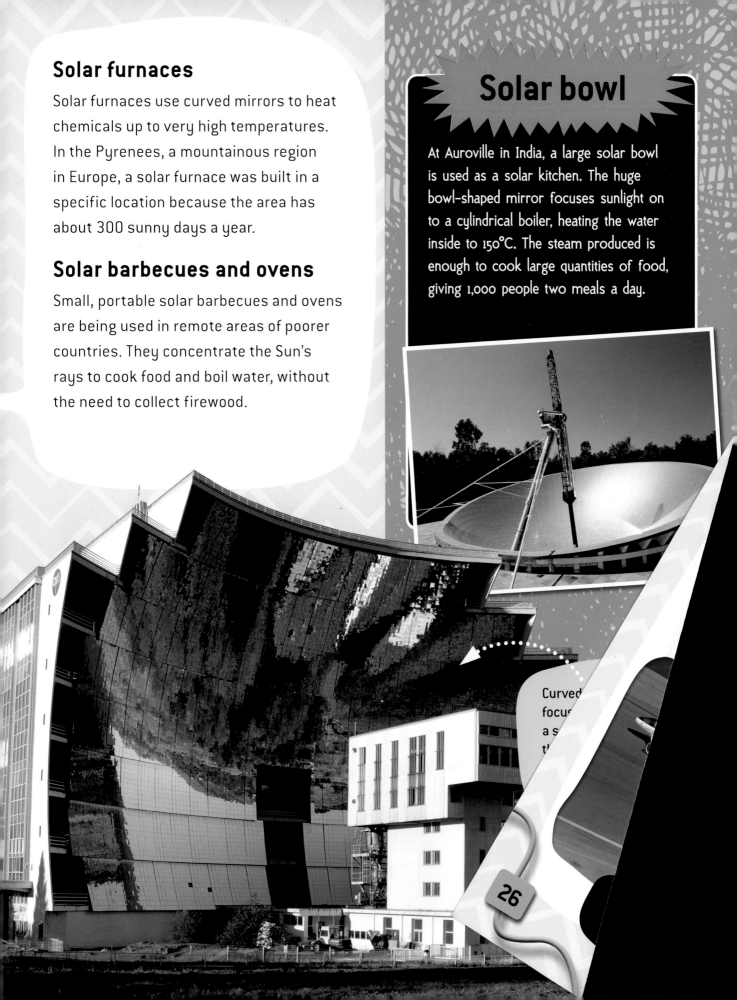

Curved
focus
a s
t

26

The future of solar energy

Solar power has a bright future. Today, most solar panels and arrays supply electricity to the home, offices and factories, but scientists and engineers are exploring all sorts of ways to make use of solar power.

Cars

The first solar-powered car appeared in 1962. It was a converted 1912 electric car with a solar panel on the roof. Since then, engineers have experimented with cars powered by the Sun and solar energy batteries that store electricity when the Sun goes in or at night. There are even solar sports car races!

Solar powered cars can reach 88 km/h.

Boats

Solar panels have been used on boats to power electrical equipment, such as radios and navigation lights. Engineers are also developing boats that have solar-powered engines rather than engines that run on petrol or diesel fuel. One of the most spectacular is *Planet Solar*. It cruised around the world, powered by a huge array of solar cells on its deck.

Trains and trams

In India, railway carriages have solar panels on the roof to power a train's lighting. Elsewhere in the world, entire trains are being designed to run on the Sun's energy, such as the *Solar Bullet* in the USA. The train will be powered by solar panels raised above the track.

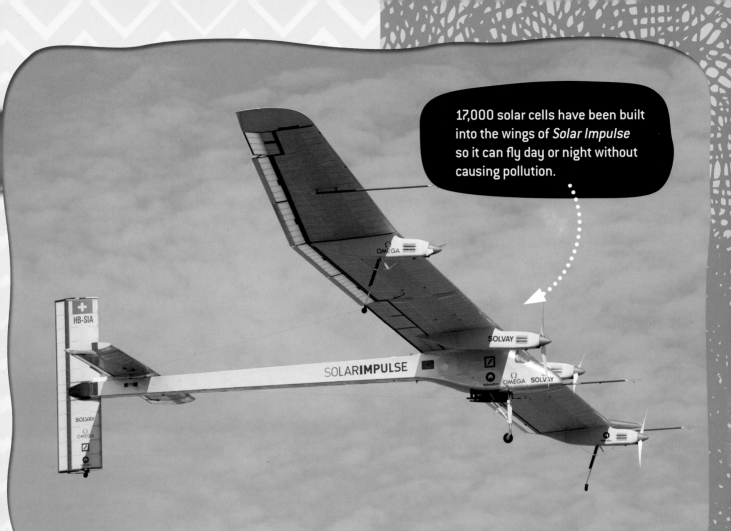

17,000 solar cells have been built into the wings of *Solar Impulse* so it can fly day or night without causing pollution.

Planes

There is even a solar-powered aeroplane! The wings of *Solar Impulse* are covered with lightweight solar panels. These drive electric motors that turn propellors. The plane has made record-breaking journeys across the world without having to use fuel or cause pollution.

Sun tower in space

Looking to the future, the ideal place to capture sunlight to generate electricity would be in space, using man-made satellites. There are no clouds to get in the way, and the satellite could be permanently facing the Sun. The electricity could be beamed down to collecting stations on Earth.

Clean energy?

There are many benefits to using solar power, but there are drawbacks as well. Decision-makers must weigh up the pros and cons.

Against solar power

* Solar power depends on the weather. The Sun is not out all of the time.

* Solar power is limited to daylight hours, unless there is the large scale storage of electricity, for example, in expensive batteries.

* Solar installations are relatively expensive and do not match the output of similar sized oil, gas, coal or nuclear power stations.

* Vast amounts of land are required for large-scale solar arrays.

* Pollution is associated with the manufacture of solar cells, such as potent 'greenhouse' gases that may have a bigger affect on climate change than carbon dioxide.

This is a traditional coal-fired power station.

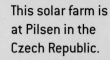

This solar farm is at Pilsen in the Czech Republic.

For solar power

* Solar power is clean and environmentally friendly.

* Solar power is renewable and sustainable. It will not run out.

* Solar power will help reduce the impact of global warming and climate change.

* Solar power generation is silent.

* The worldwide potential is enormous. Each year, solar energy could deliver up to 90 times the current annual energy use of the entire world.

Copying the Sun

Some energy scientists dream of copying the way the Sun works here on Earth. Current nuclear power stations work by generating heat from splitting the atom, a process called 'fission', but the by-product is hazardous radioactive waste. If scientists can join atoms, a process called 'fusion', which is what goes on inside the Sun, large scale energy production would be cleaner and safer than nuclear power generation. The problem is, fusion power is very difficult to achieve.

Leading the way

Solar power may not be the cleanest form of electricity generation, but it is cleaner than oil, gas, coal and nuclear power. With more people turning to renewable energy and more countries determined to lower their use of fossil fuels, solar energy could be a leading way to generate electricity. The International Energy Agency predicts that by 2060 it could account for a third of the world's energy needs.

Glossary

absorb To take in or soak up

air conditioning A system to change the quality of the air in a building

alternating current An electric current that reverses its direction many times a second

atmosphere The air that surrounds the Earth

atom The smallest part of a chemical element that can exist

circuit breaker An automatic device for stopping the flow of electricity

climate change A change in global climate patterns largely due to high levels of carbon dioxide in the atmosphere

converted Changed

direct current An electric current flowing in one direction only

distribution line The cable that carries electricity around the country

electric field A region with a force generated by electricity

equator An imaginary line drawn around the Earth which is the same distance from both poles

filament A thin wire in a light bulb

fossil fuel A fuel made from the remains of ancient plants and animals

fuse A safety device in which a filament melts and breaks an electric circuit if the current exceeds a safe level

generate To produce or create

global warming An increase in the global temperature due mainly to increased levels of carbon dioxide in the atmosphere

hydroelectric power The generation of electricity from the movement of water

insulated Describes something separated by a material that prevents heat, electricity or sound leaking out

mains The main distribution system for electrical power in a building

plasma A form of gas at very high temperatures, such as in the Sun's core

radioactive waste Any material contaminated by radioactivity

reservoir An artificial lake to store water

subatomic particle The unit of matter smaller than a hydrogen atom

turbine A machine in which a wheel fitted with fins is made to revolve in a fast-moving stream of air, steam, water or gas

vacuum A space without any matter

voltage A measure of the electrical force that would drive an electric current between two points

Further information

BOOKS

Eco-Works: How a Solar-Powered Home Works
by Robyn Hardyman, Franklin Watts 2015

Eco-Works: How Renewable Energy Works
by Geoff Barker, Franklin Watts 2015

Straight Forward with Science: Electricity
by Peter Riley, Franklin Watts 2015

The World of Infographics: Natural Resources
by Jon Richards and Ed Simkins, Wayland 2014

WEBSITES

Visit this website for fun facts about solar power:
http://www.funkidslive.com/features/curious-kate/curious-facts-about-solar-power/

The BBC Bitesize webpage will give you lots of information about solar energy:
http://www.bbc.co.uk/schools/gcsebitesize/science/aqa_pre_2011/energy/mainselectricityrev6.shtml

More facts about renewable energy sources:
http://www.alliantenergykids.com/energyandtheenvironment/renewableenergy/022403

Index

First published in Great Britain in 2016 by Wayland
Copyright © Wayland, 2016

All rights reserved.

Author: Michael Bright
Freelance editor: Katie Woolley
Editors: Annabel Stones and Liza Miller
Designer: Rocket Design (East Anglia) Ltd

ISBN: 9780750296496
10 9 8 7 6 5 4 3 2 1

Wayland
An imprint of
Hachette Children's Group
Part of Hodder & Stoughton
Carmelite House
50 Victoria Embankment
London EC4Y 0DZ

An Hachette UK Company
www.hachette.co.uk
www.hachettechildrens.co.uk

Printed in China

Illustrations by Stefan Chabluk: 2–3, 6, 14–15

Picture credits:
All images and graphic elements courtesy of Shutterstock except:
Science Photo Library. 9tl & 11b: NASA. 13t: View Pictures/Getty. 16: NASA. 17t: Jochen Tack/imageBROKER/Corbis. 19t: Perry Mastrovito/Corbis. 23b: Yann Arthus-Bertrand/Corbis. 25t: Chris Hellier/Corbis. 25b: Floris Leeuwenberg/The Cover Story/Corbis. 26: George Tiedemann/Corbis.

Every effort has been made to clear copyright. Should there be any inadvertent omission, please apply to the publisher for rectification.

The website addresses (URLs) included in this book were valid at the time of going to press. However, it is possible that contents or addresses may have changed since the publication of this book. No responsibility for any such changes can be accepted by either the author or the Publisher.

MIX
Paper from responsible sources
FSC® C104740
FSC
www.fsc.org

source to resource

The four books in the Source to Resource series examine Earth's most important resources. They support the geography curriculum and are designed to encourage readers to debate some of today's most pressing environmental issues.

FROM **FIELD** TO **PLATE**

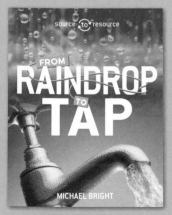

978 0 7502 9645 8

FROM **OIL RIG** TO **PETROL PUMP**

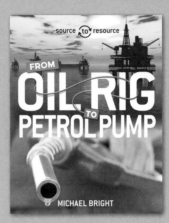

978 0 7502 9648 9

FROM **RAINDROP** TO **TAP**

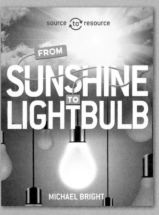

978 0 7502 9650 2

FROM **SUNSHINE** TO **LIGHTBULB**

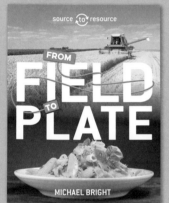

978 0 7502 9649 6